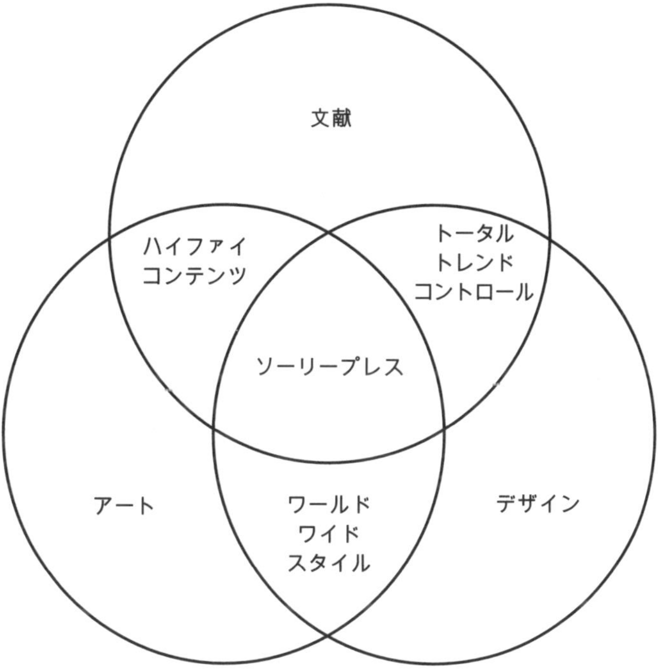

www.sorry-press.com

Stefan Marx, geboren 1979, ist ein deutscher Zeichner.
Er lebt und arbeitet in Berlin.

1979年生まれのステファン・マルクスはドイツの絵描きです。
彼はベルリンに住み、働いています。

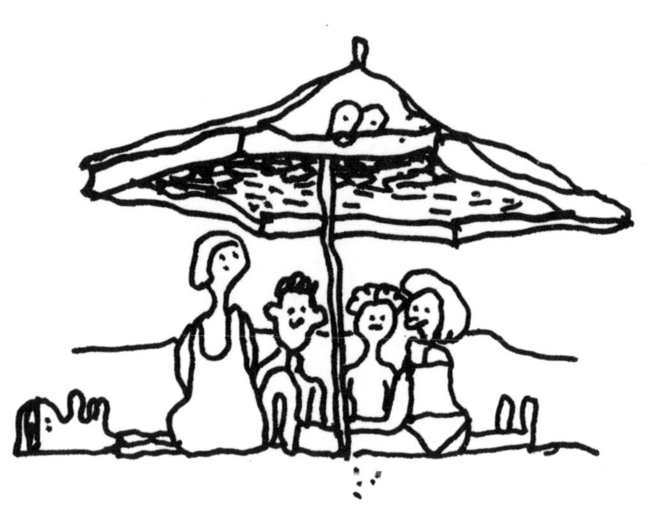

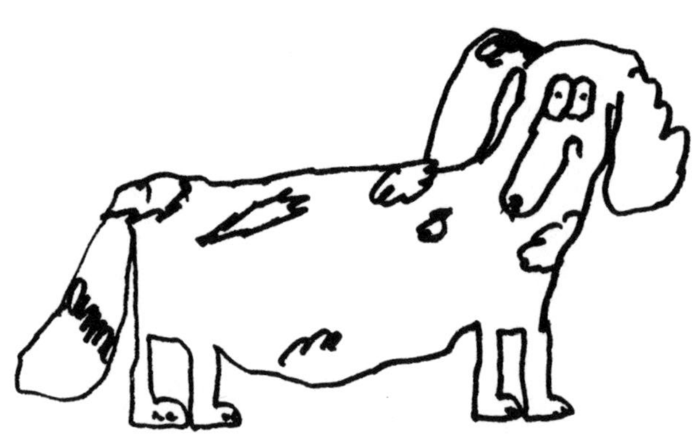

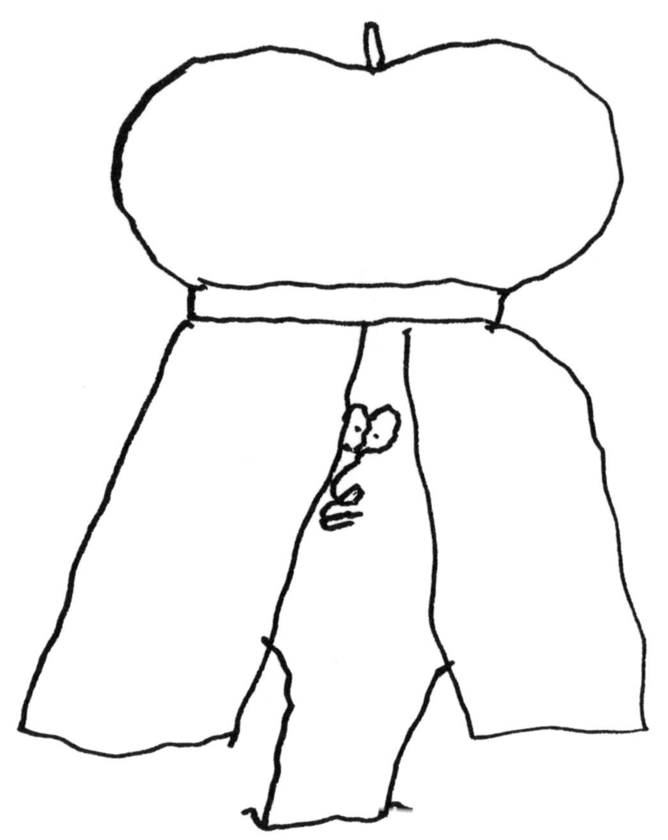

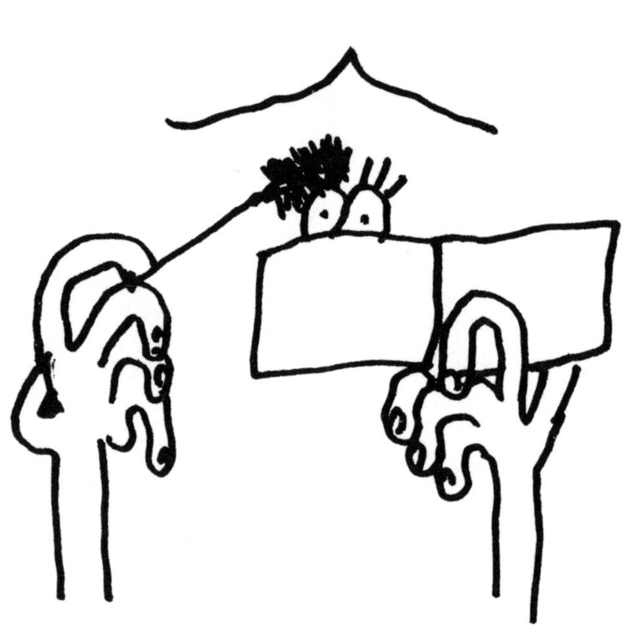

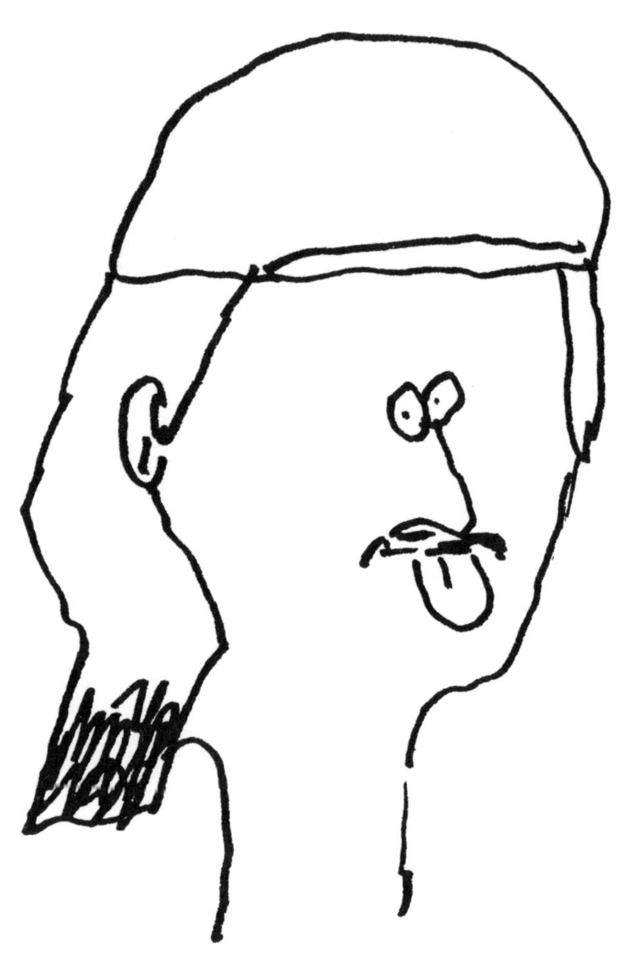

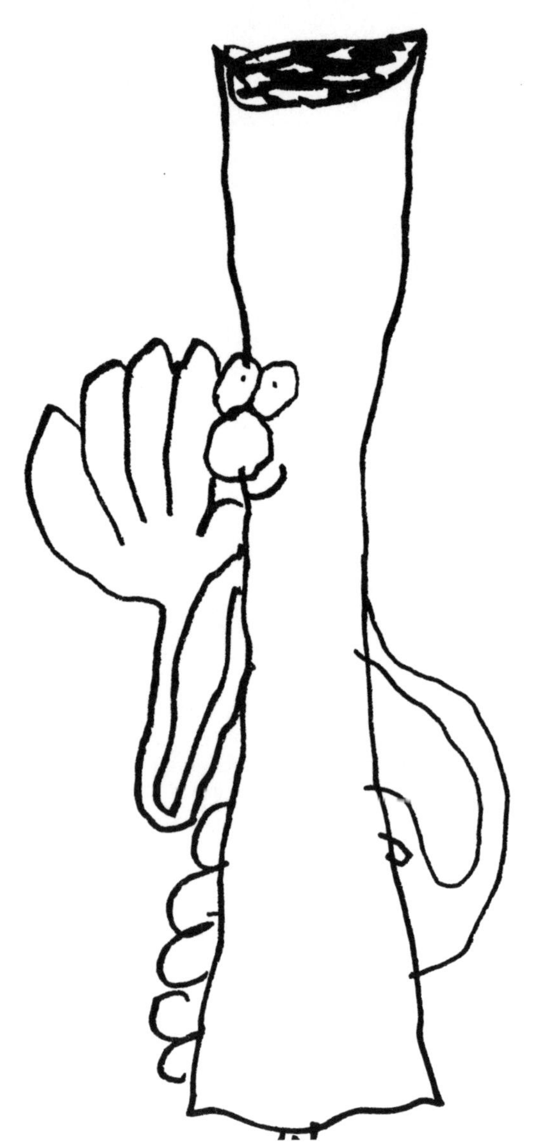

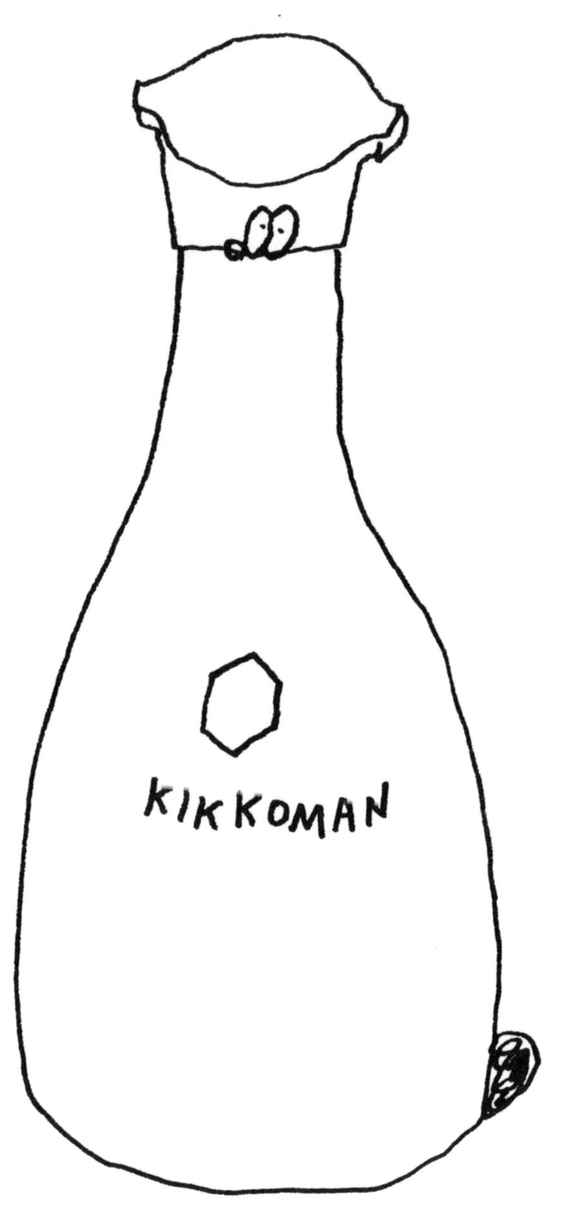

KIKKOMAN

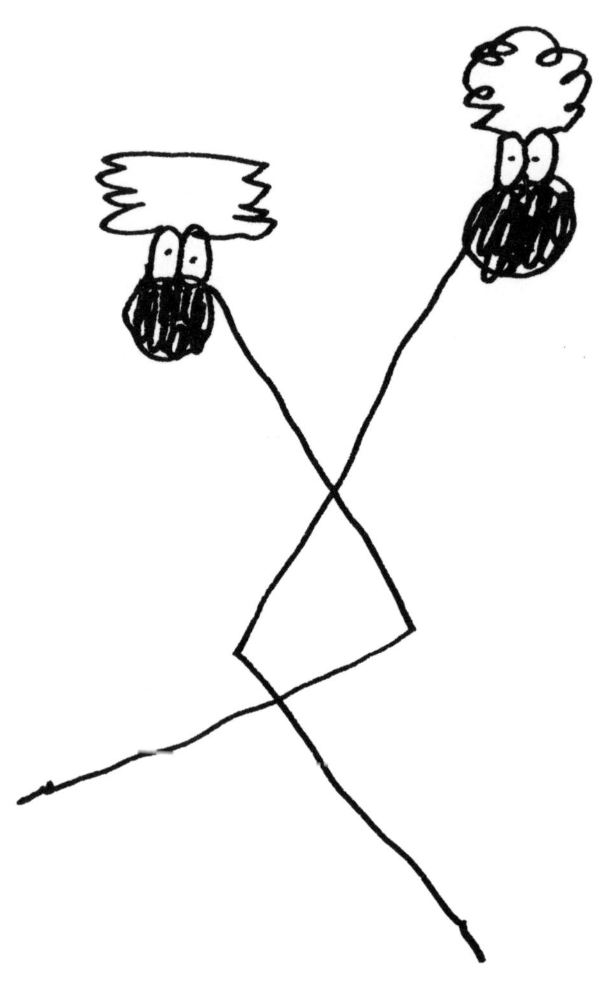

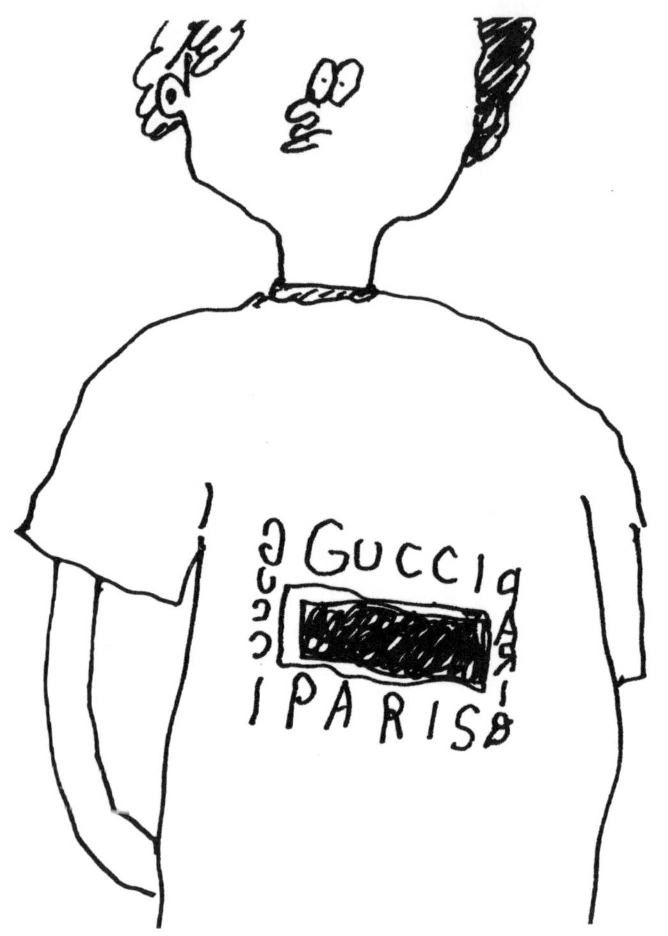

Guccia
PARIS

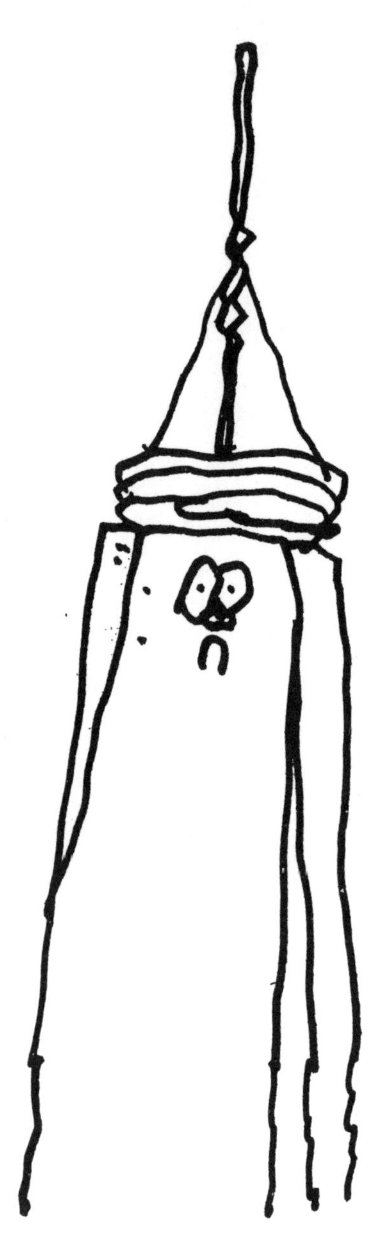

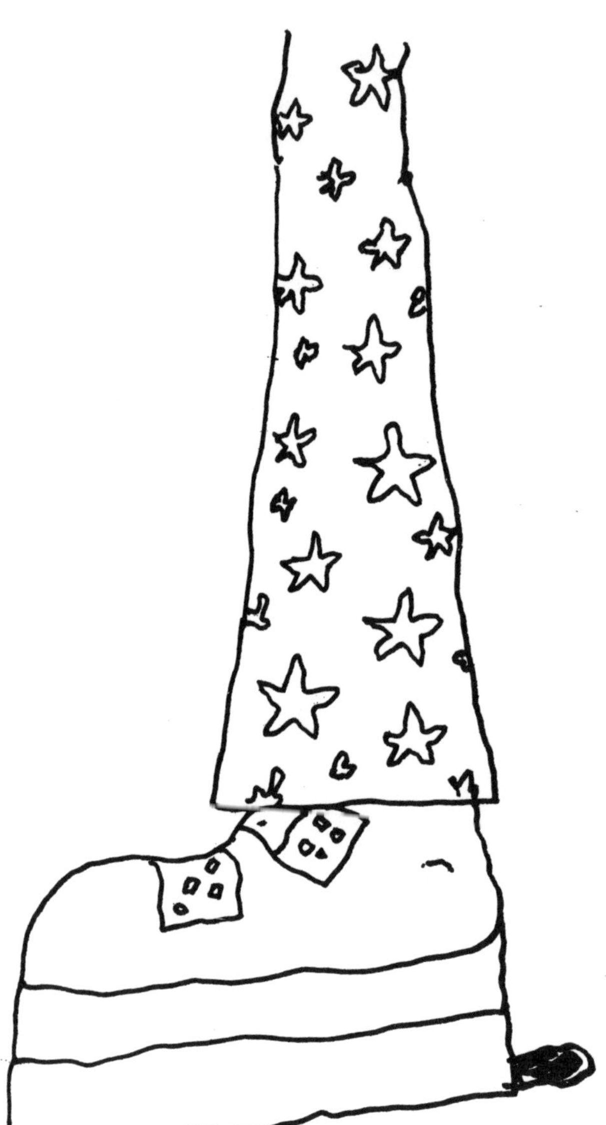

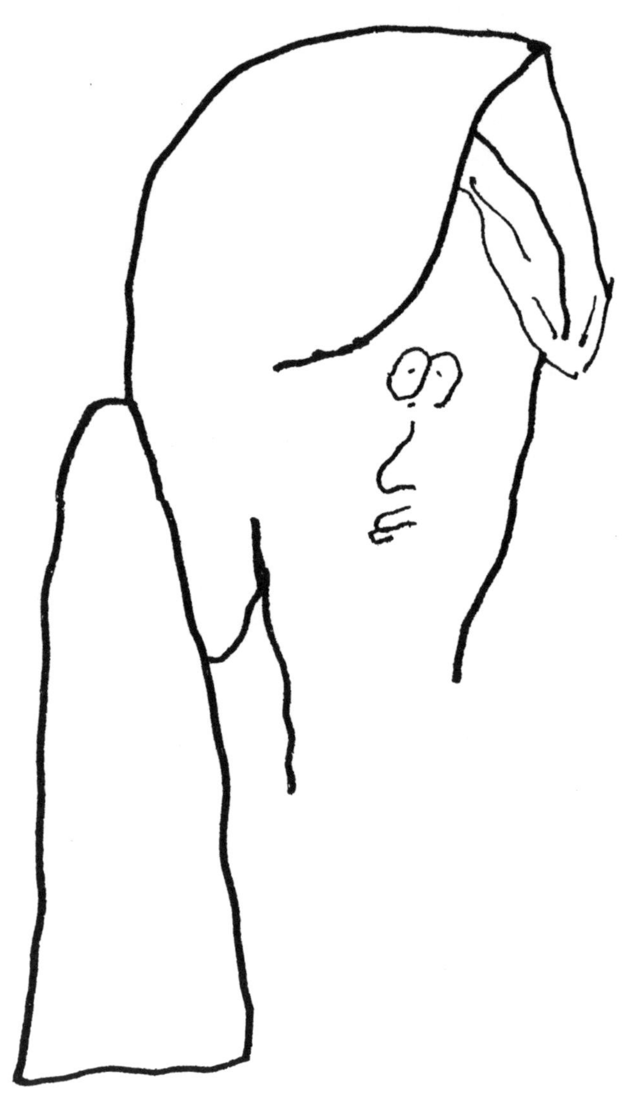

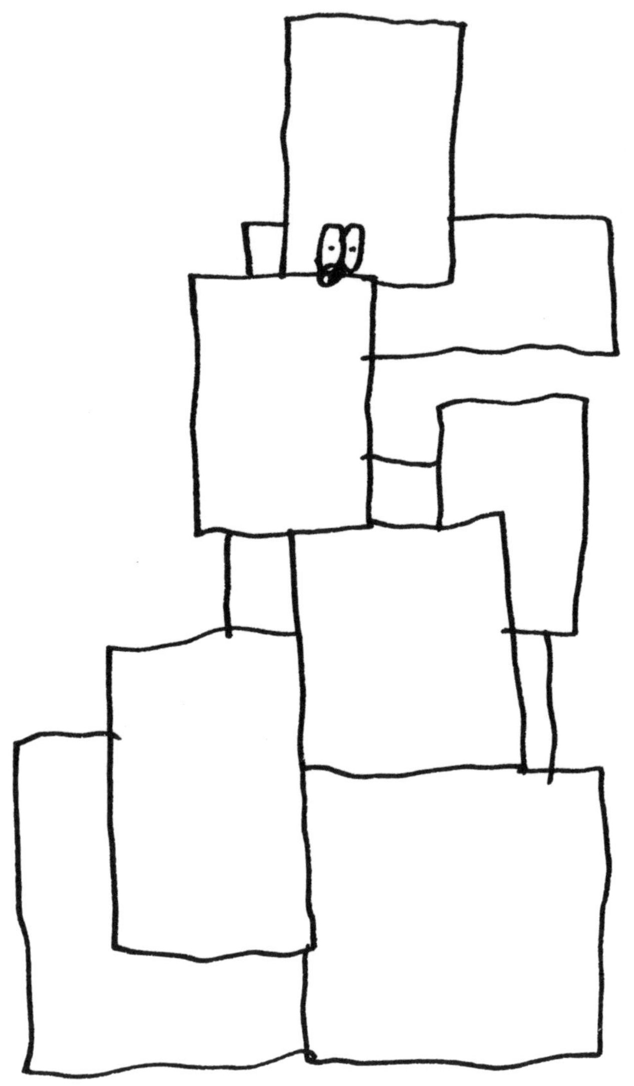

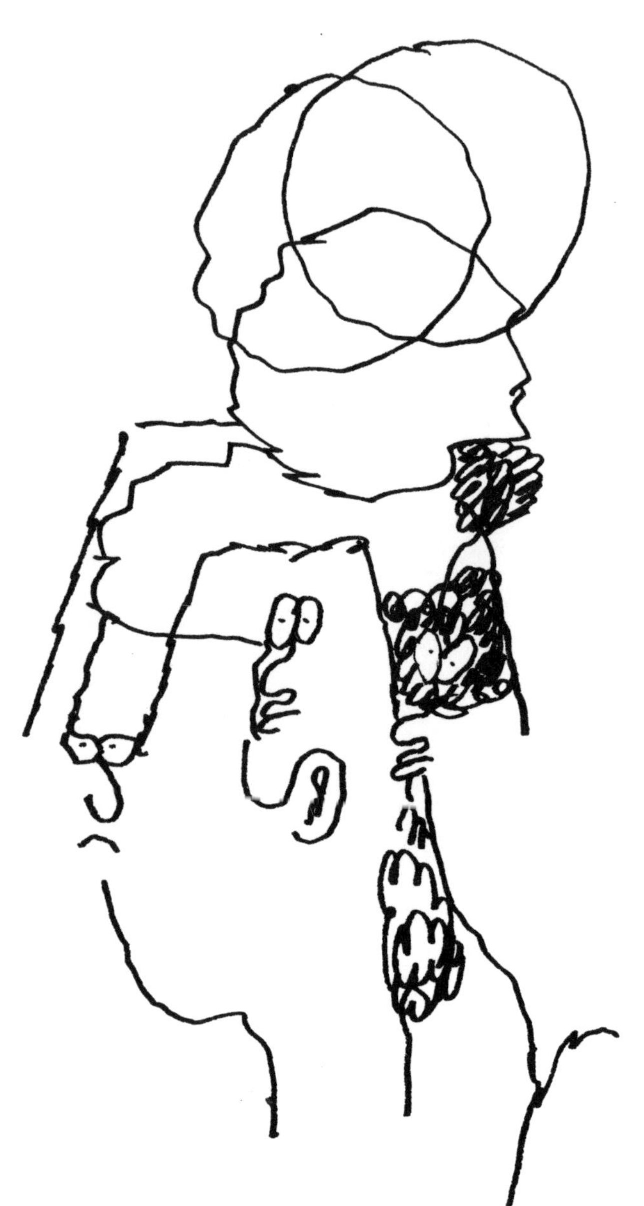

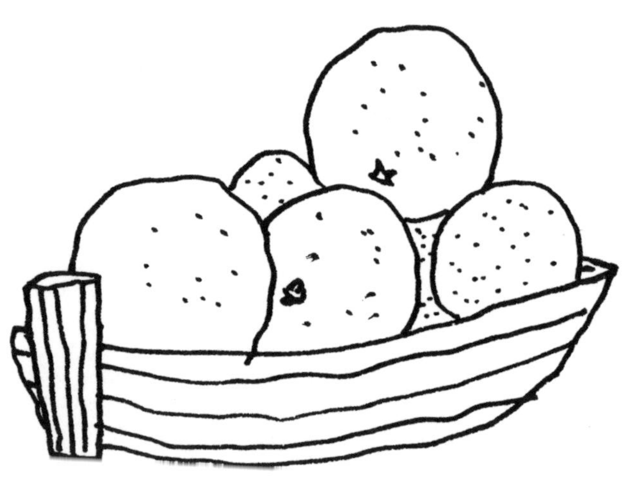

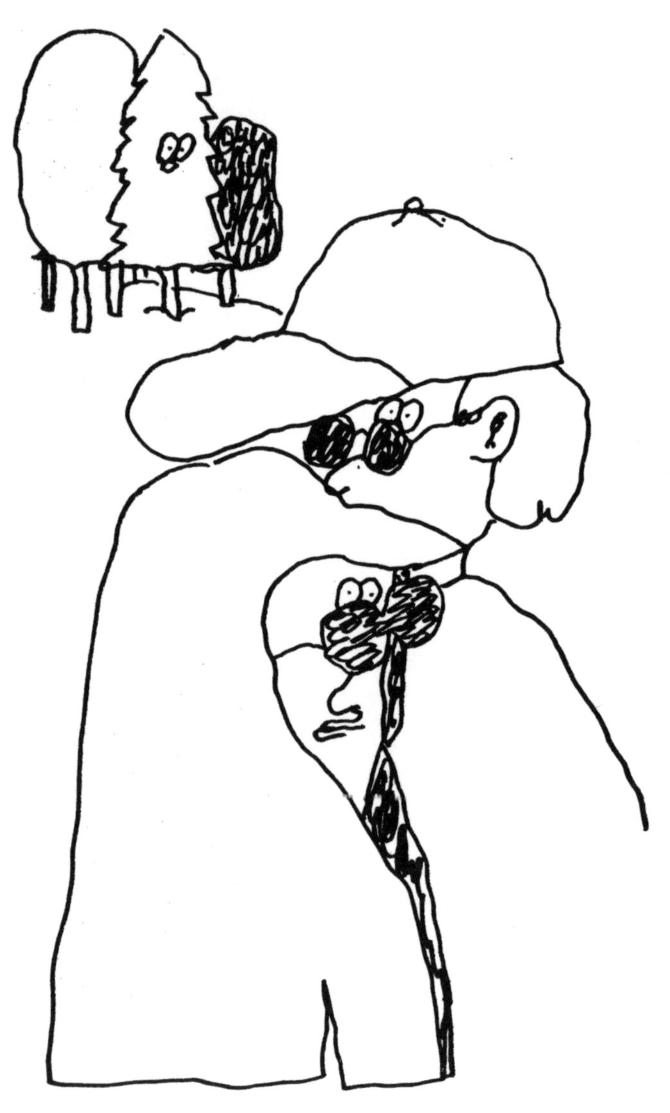

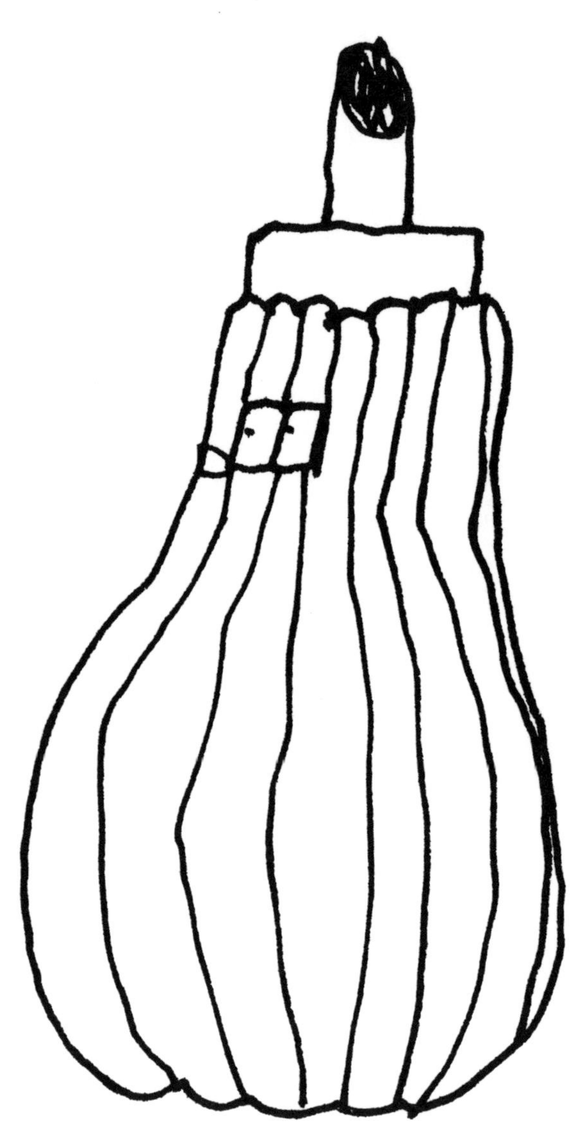

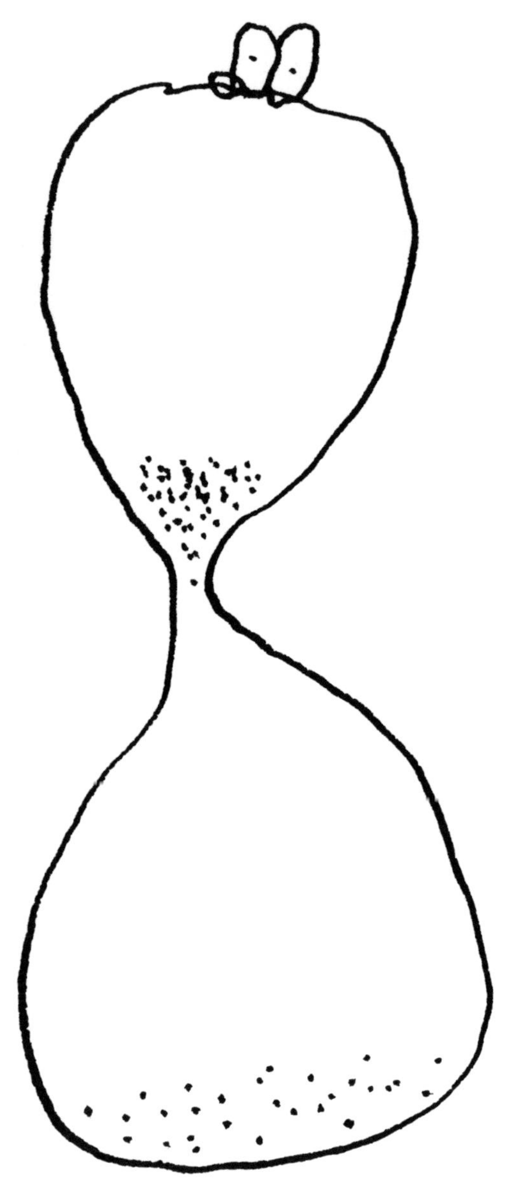

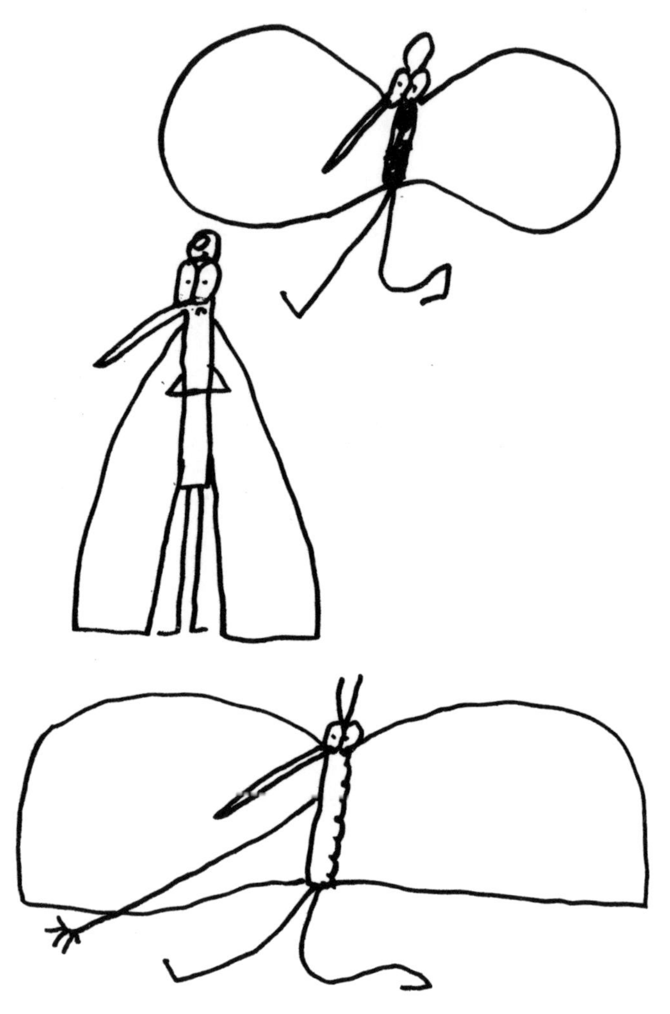

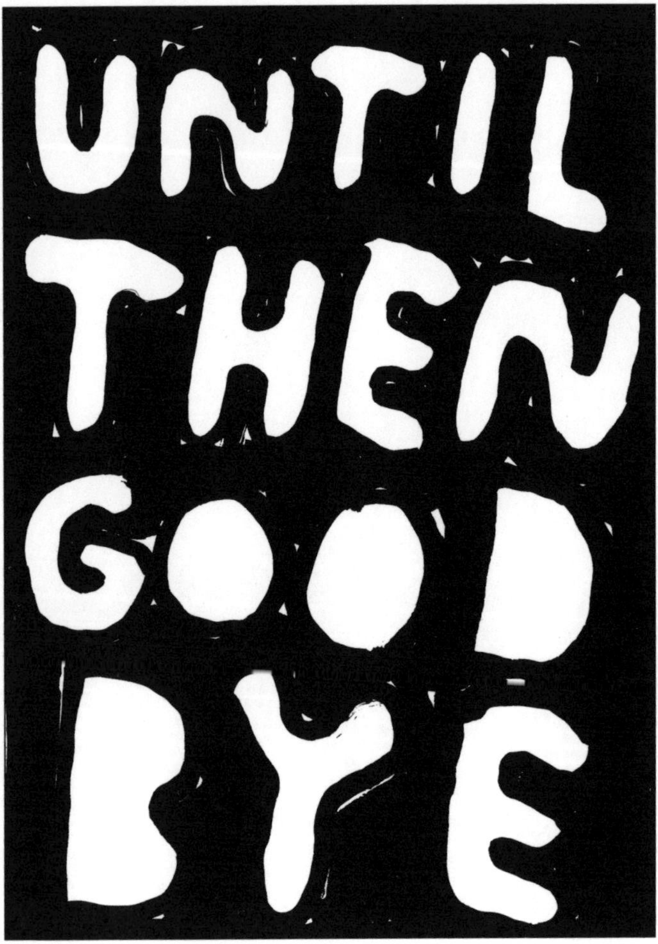

UNTIL
THEN
GOOD
BYE

THIS
IS SO
NOT
WHAT I
WANTED

RARE FEELINGS

MUST
BE
ANOTHER
ONE

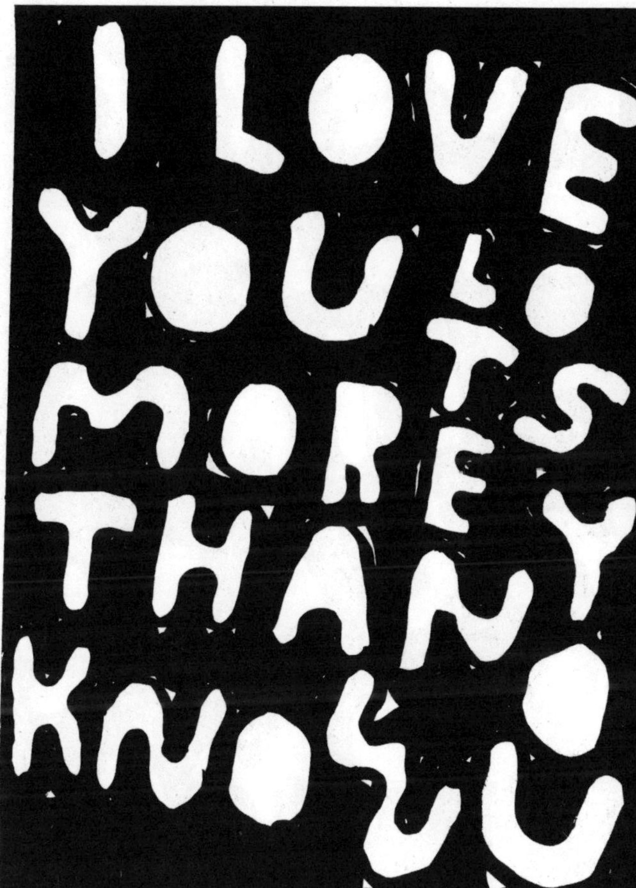

I LOVE
YOU
LOTS
MORE
THAN
KNOW U

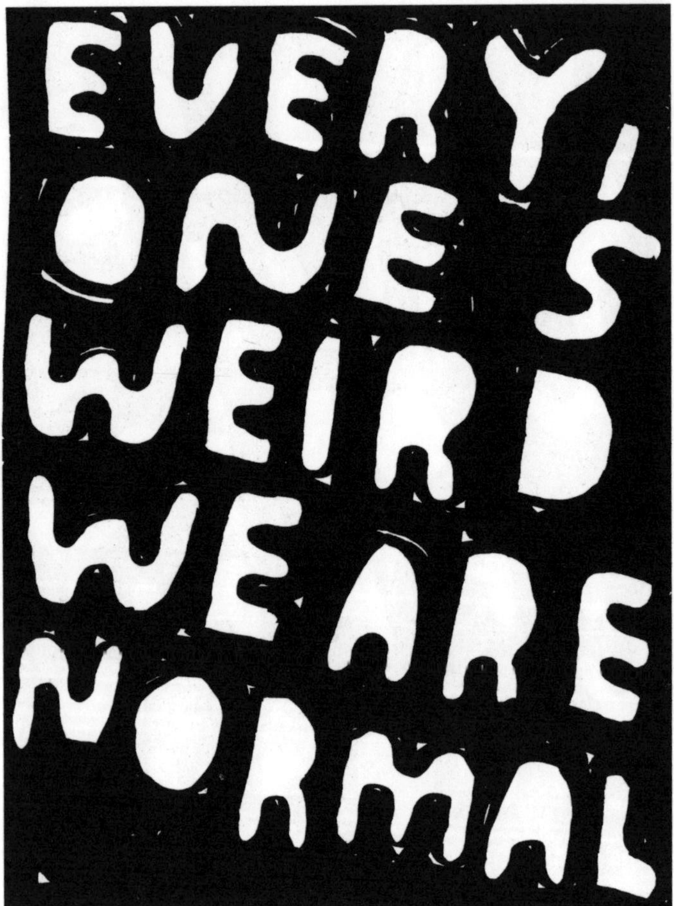

EVERY
ONE'S
WEIRD
WE ARE
NORMAL

BECAUSE YOU ARE EMPTY AND I AM EMPTY

DROPOFF
AM

PICKUP
PM

DROP OFF
PM
PICKUP
AM

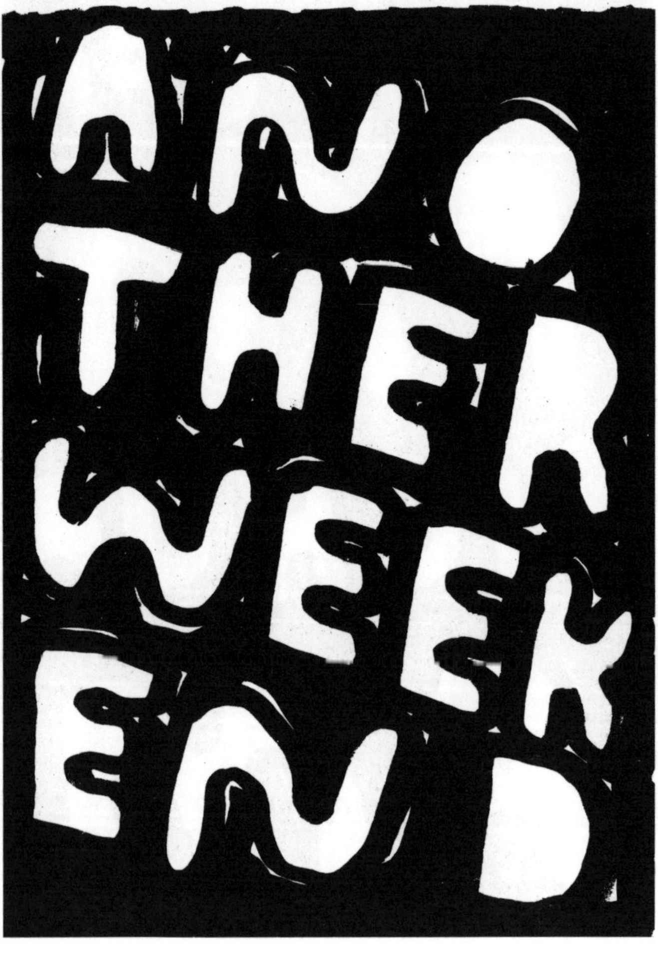

ANOTHER WEEKEND

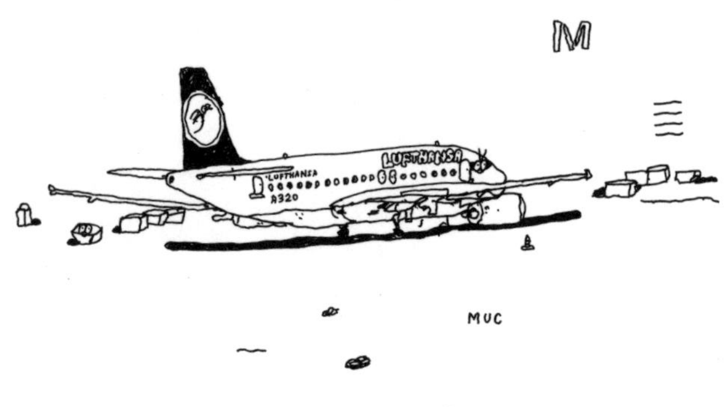
M
LUFTHANSA
LUFTHANSA
A320
MUC

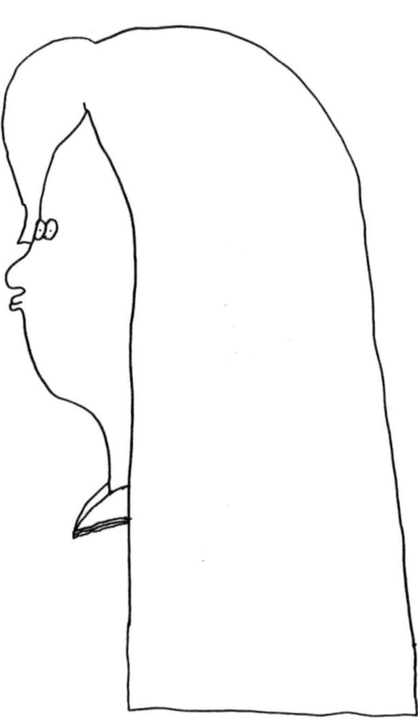

GATE
3

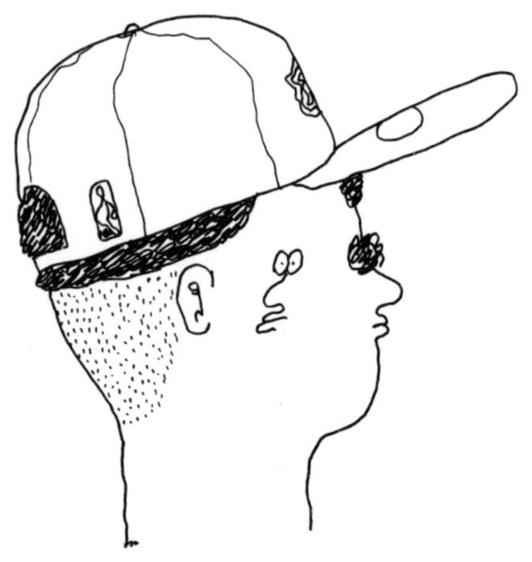

LAST
&
FINAL

BOARDING

CALL

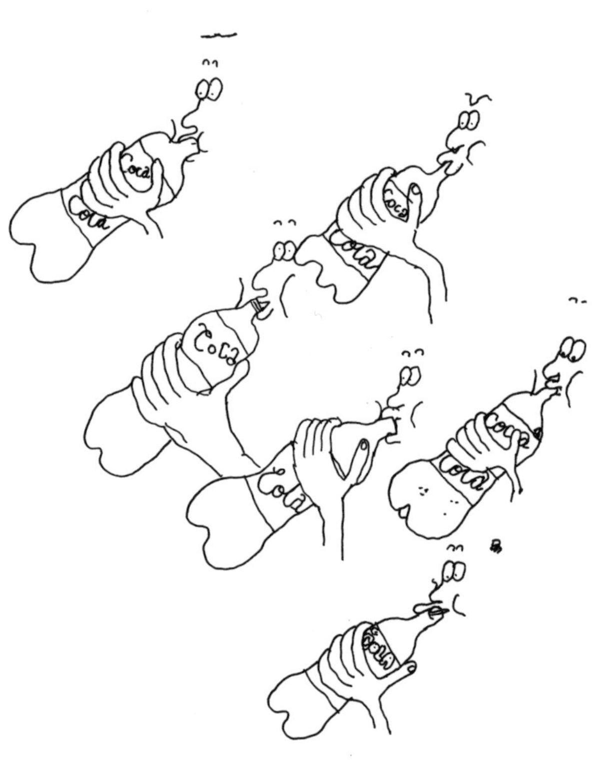

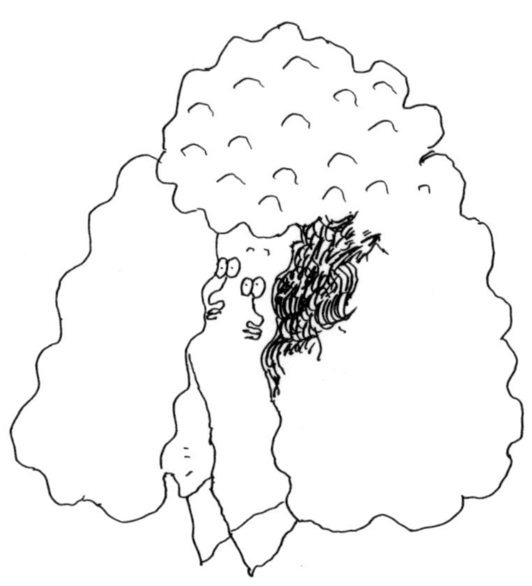

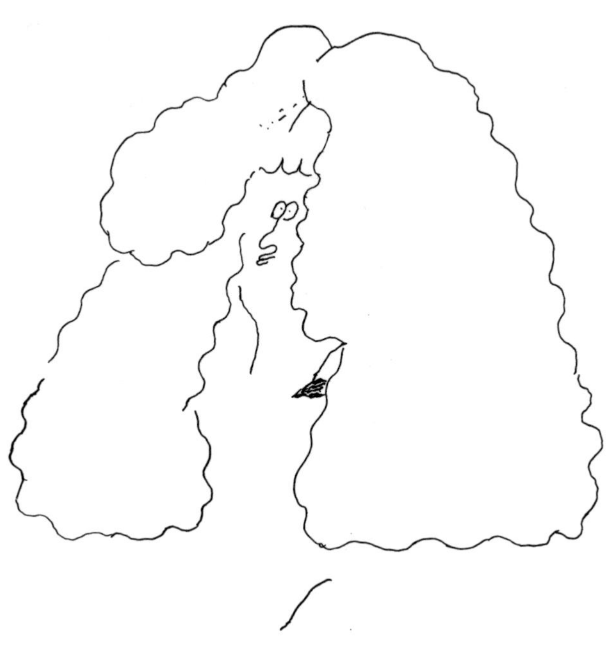

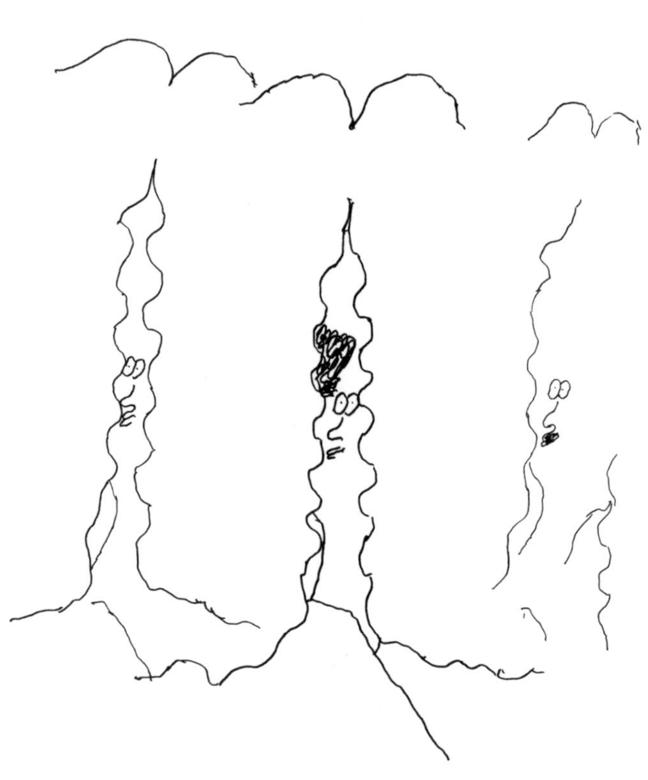

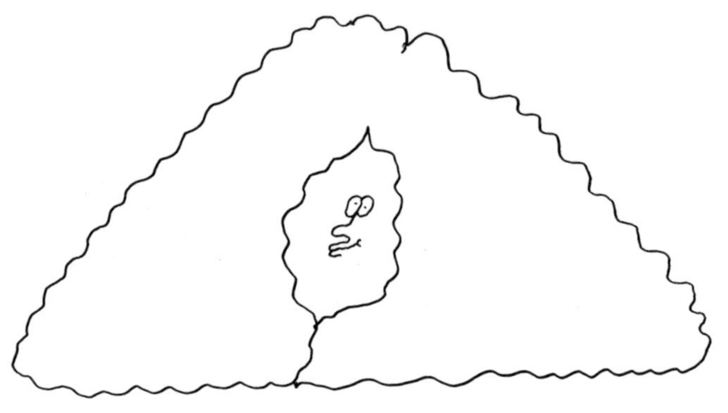

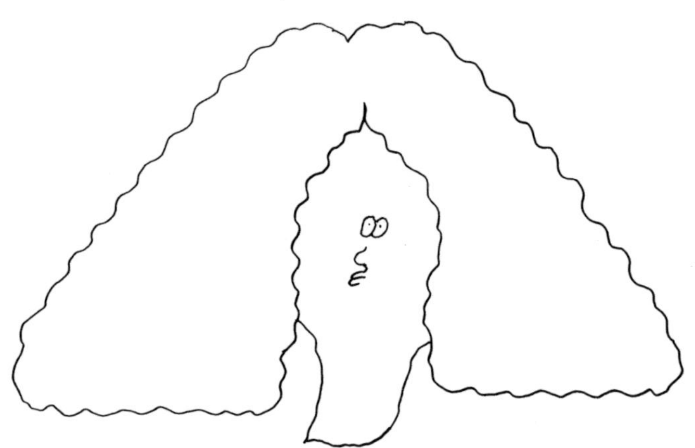

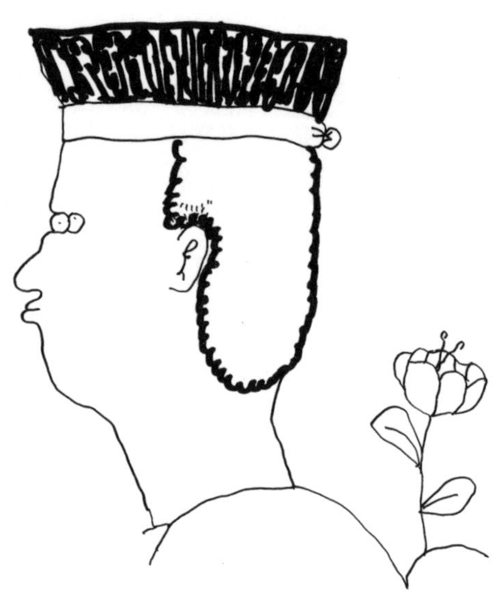

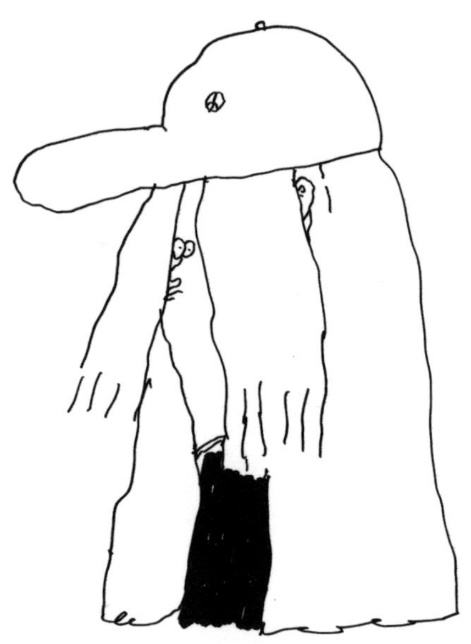

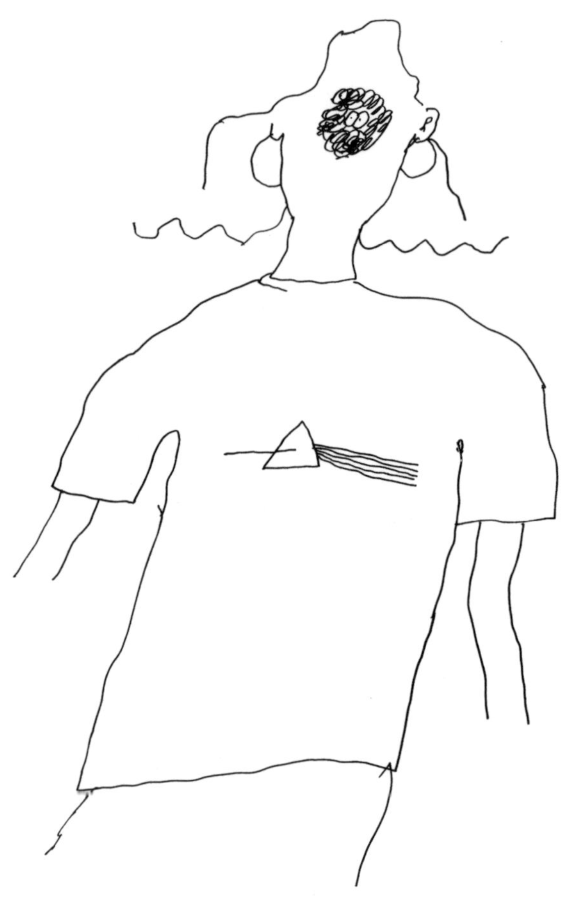

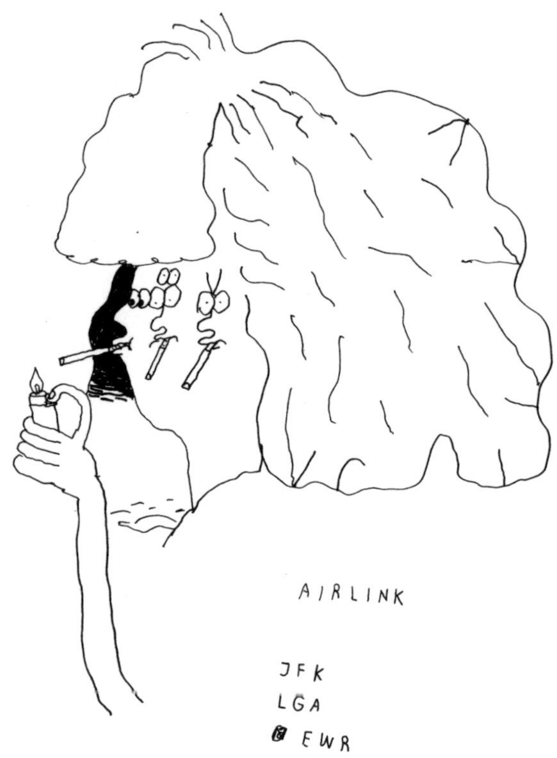

AIRLINK
JFK
LGA
EWR

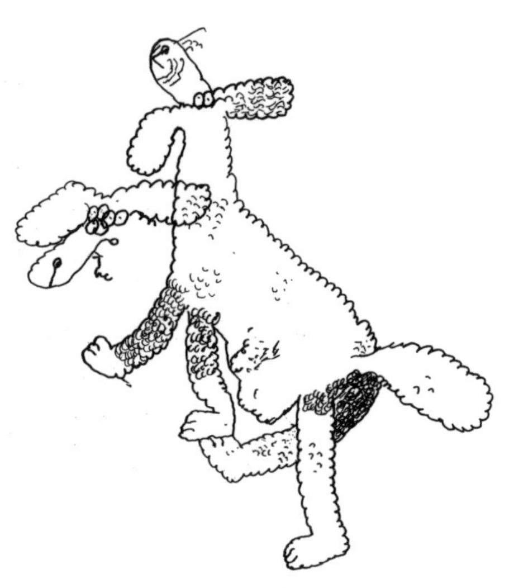

FLAT FARE

JFK

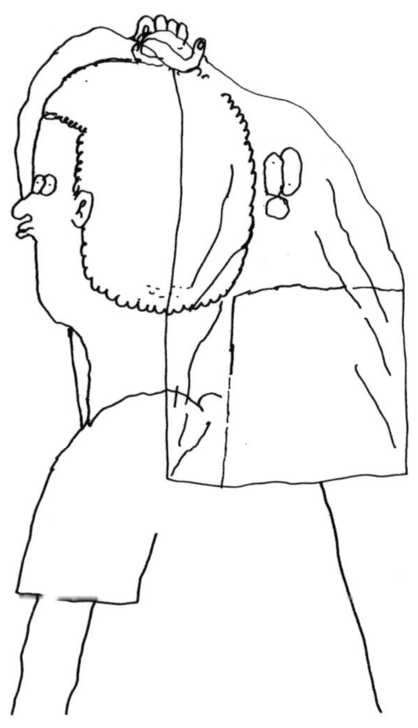

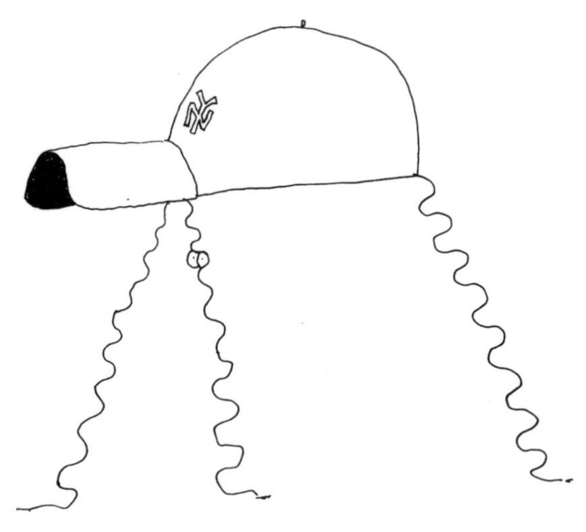

NEED CASH ATM

BROOME ST ORCHARD ST

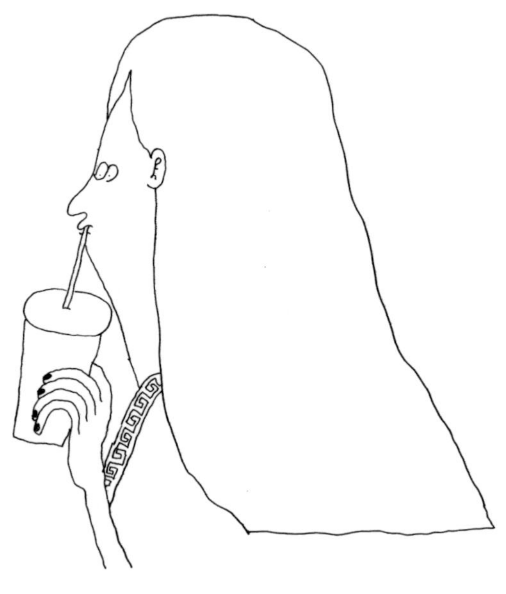

ONE WAY

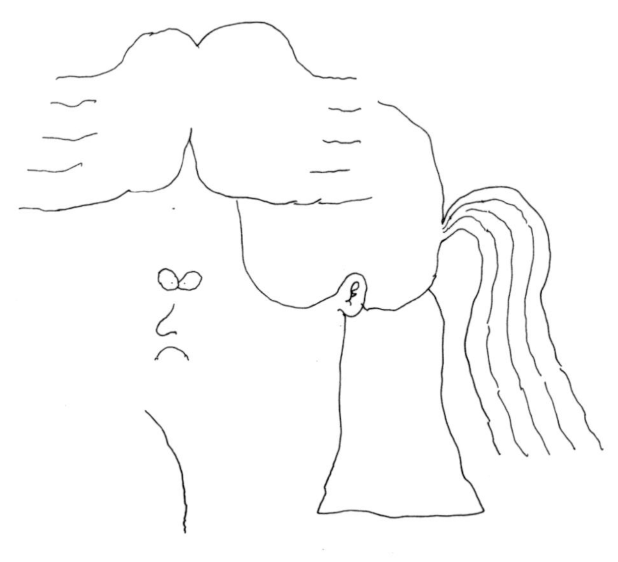

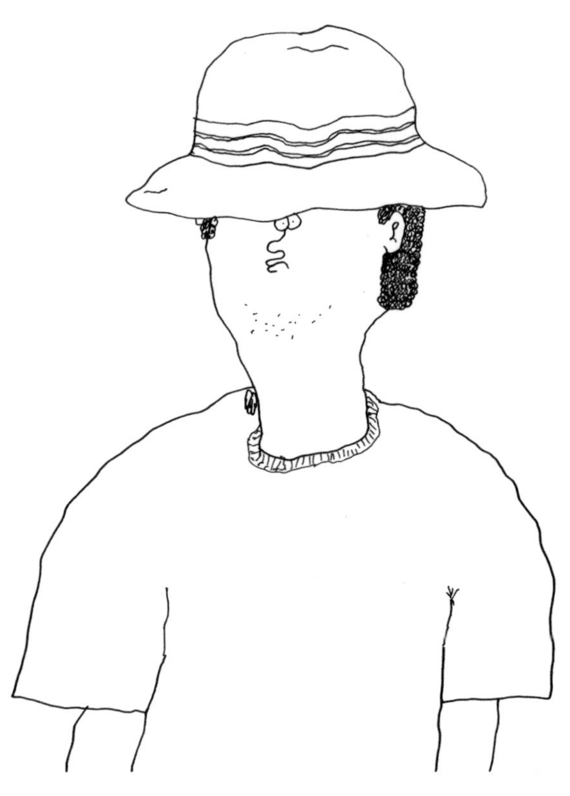

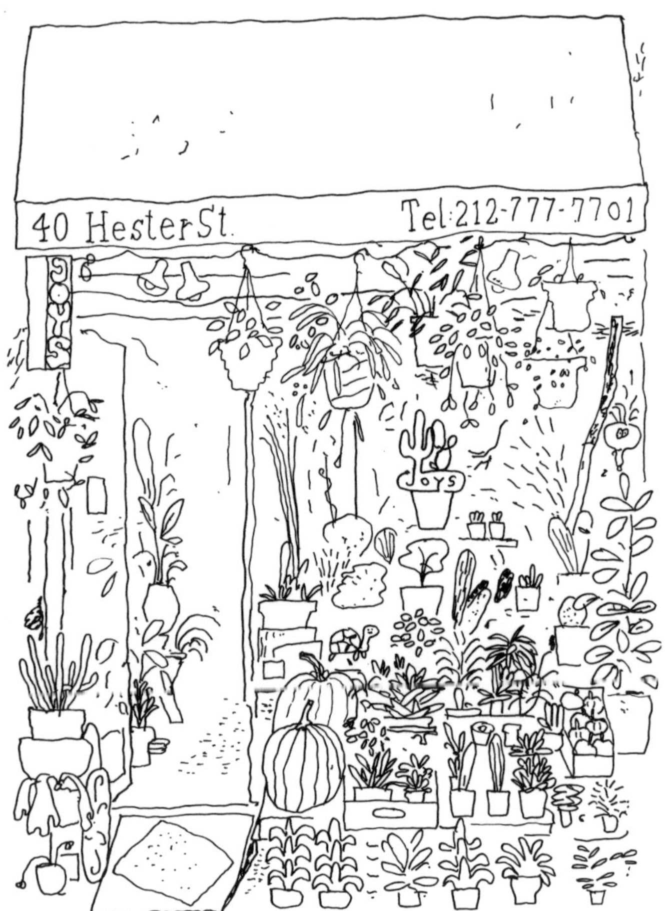

40 HesterSt.
Tel:212-777-7701
JOYS

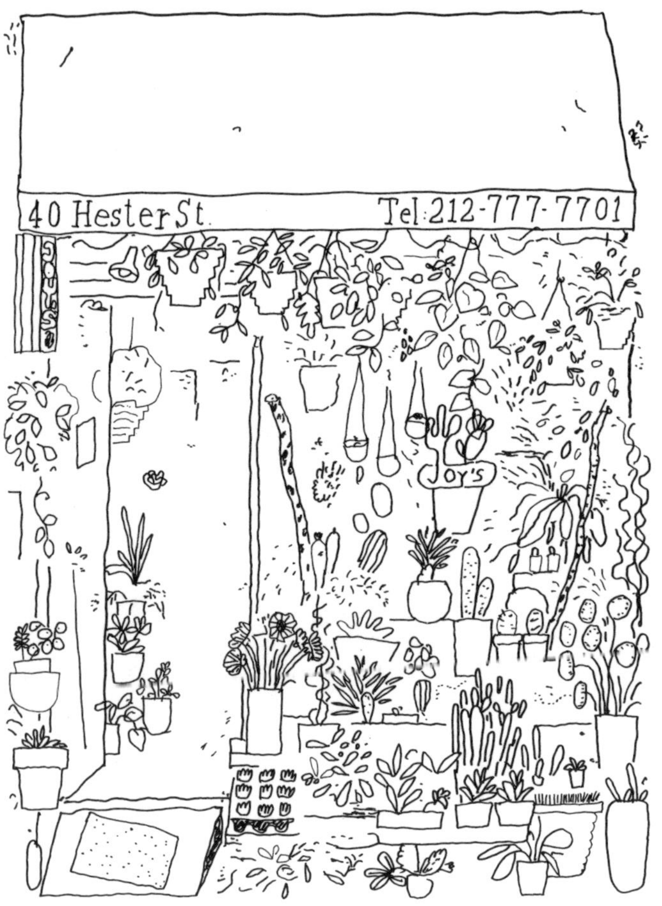

40 Hester St.
Tel: 212-777-7701
Joy's

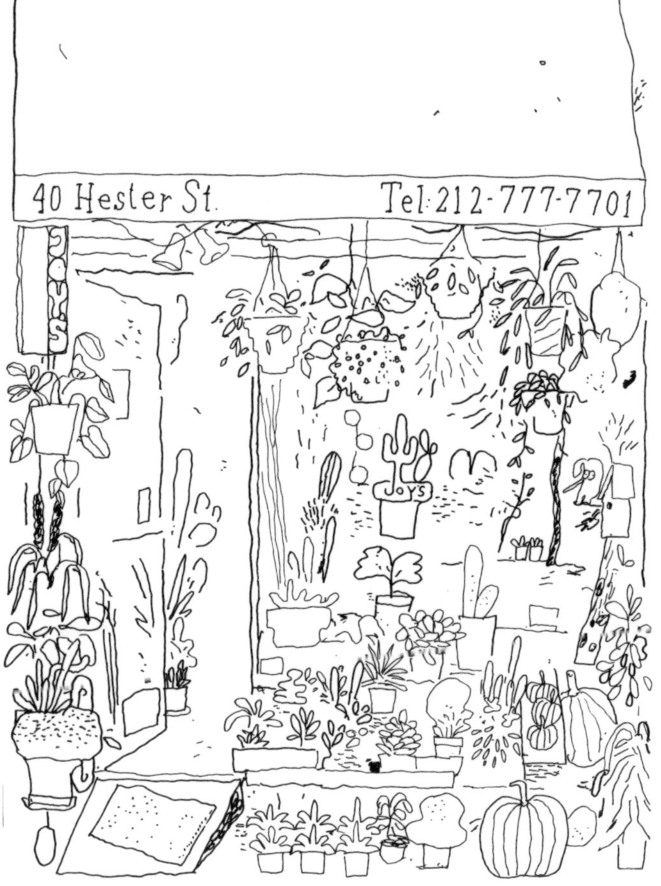

40 Hester St.
Tel: 212-777-7701
JOY'S
JOY'S

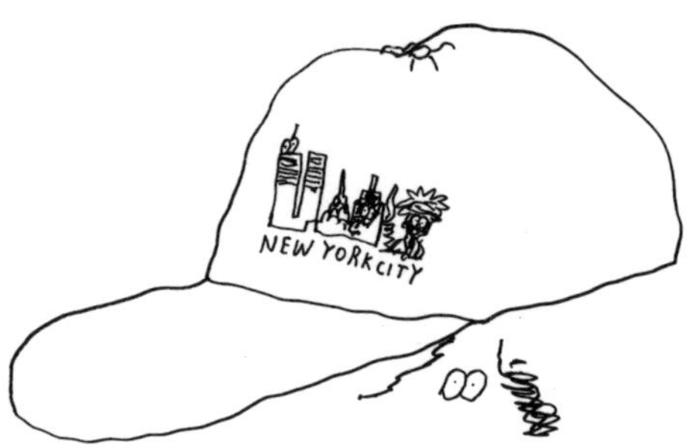

NEW YORK CITY

Stefan Marx
Das Kapitel / 章
Japan Edition / 日本版
© Sorry Press München 2020
© ソーリープレス ミュンヘン 2020
Lukas Kubina & Moritz Wiegand
Zeichnungen / 素描: © Stefan Marx
Design / 設計: Wiegand von Hartmann GbR
Druck / 印刷: Stückle Druck
Printed in Germany / ドイツで印刷
ISBN 978-3-9820440-5-7